A Room Inside My Mind

An Intimate Archive Of What Remained

Spencer Vincent Verdecchio

BookLeaf Publishing
India | USA | UK

Made with ❤ on the BookLeaf Publishing Platform
www.bookleafpub.in
www.bookleafpub.com

Dedication

For those I hurt when I was hurting.

For those who loved me at my worst.

For Mr. Ritter & Ms. Barry.

For Rania, always. <3

Acknowledgement

To those who have loved me through the darkest rooms in my mind— thank you.
Thank you for seeing me when I couldn't see myself,
for holding space when I couldn't speak,
and for reminding me that my softness was never a weakness.
Your love has been the quiet light
guiding me back to myself
again and again.

To my best friend, Rania—
you have been the most steady thing in my life.
A constant when everything else shifted.
A calm presence in the chaos,
never asking me to be anything other than who I am.
You inspire me every single day to show up fully to life.
I hope you know that your love lives in every corner of my being.

To everyone who has stayed, who has listened,
who has chosen me even in silence—
this book exists because you made it safe
for me to speak again.

With all the love I didn't always know how to show,
— Spencer Vincent

Preface

This book is not a beginning—
it's a return.

Some of these poems were written decades ago,
when I had no language
for the heaviness I carried.
Others were written recently,
with hands steadier,
but still shaking.

Each piece comes from somewhere
I didn't always have the courage to name.
They were written in the quiet,
in the dark,
in the aftermath.

What lives inside these pages
isn't polished or perfect—
it's real.
It's raw.
It's what remained

when everything else fell away.

I've walked through years of silence
to get here—
to give shape
to the things that almost swallowed me.
And now I offer them to you.
Not for answers,
not for praise—
but as proof
that even the most fractured rooms
can hold something
honest
and whole.

If you find yourself somewhere in these words—
in the ache,
the longing,
the slow return to self—
know that you're not alone.
There is space for you here.
There always was.

— Spencer Vincent

The Room With No Door

There was a summer
where time warped—
days heavy with heat,
nights that hummed
with unease.

A threshold I didn't mean to cross
appeared without warning—
and once inside,
the air changed.
The walls didn't speak...
but they remembered.

I left parts of myself there—
not all at once, but in the slow ways
you lose things without realizing.

At first, I called it a dream,
something half-formed
by shadows and sleep.
But it followed me

into waking.
It shaped the way I opened,
the way I closed,
the way I flinched
when no one even
touched me.

I learned to vanish
without leaving.
To fold myself small
in rooms that never asked,
Why?

Years later,
I tried to speak it
into something real—
but truth
when inconvenient,
is often called a lie.

Now, I carry that room
beneath the noise.
It has no windows,
no exit,
no name—

only memory,
only breath,
only the wonder
of who I might've been
if I never entered.

Passenger

It started as something
I let ride beside me—
quiet, unassuming,
a presence I could ignore
when the sun was out
and my hands were full.

But on days when everything
felt too loud, too heavy,
too sharp around the edges,
I let it take the wheel.

It knew the roads I didn't.
Promised shortcuts
through my own mind.
Told me I could sleep
while it steered.

And I believed it.
Because peace—
even while borrowed,
felt better than drowning awake.

But I didn't notice
when the scenery stopped changing.
Didn't realize we were driving in circles
until the gas ran out and I
didn't know how to walk back home.

By then,
I had forgotten
how to sit still
without it.

And even now,
long after I've taken back the keys,
I sometimes catch it
in the rearview mirror—
still smiling,
still waiting,
still pretending
it ever knew the way.

Afterman

Nothing was the same after you left.
It felt as if the sun started rising from west
and setting to the east.
The world didn't fall apart—
it just turned upside down
in a way no one else seemed to notice.

I'd walk into rooms
and forget why I was there.
Not in a distracted way—
more like my body had arrived
but my sense of purpose hadn't.
Even my reflection looked misplaced,
as if I'd borrowed my face
from someone else
and couldn't remember how to return it.

The coffee tasted off,
but I kept drinking it.
Mornings felt like evenings,
and nights dragged on
like they were waiting

for me to become someone
worth keeping.

I started talking to the wind,
because it was the only thing
that moved through me
without asking for anything back.

You were a map I memorized too well—
every turn,
every landmark,
etched into me
until I forgot
how to travel without you.

And when you left,
I wasn't lost.
I was emptied.
Like a house
where someone once lived
and left everything in boxes,
labeled but unopened.

I've been unpacking ever since.

Eggshells

I learned early
how to balance
on a floor
that creaked with every breath.
How to tiptoe through a house
that never asked for noise,
only silence
and unspoken apologies.

I became a weather reader—
watching the sky behind your eyes
for signs of storm.
Some days,
my presence felt like pressure.
Like too much weight
on something already cracking.

I don't remember
being light.
Only being careful.
Careful with my voice,
with my needs,

with the way I closed doors
too softly to be noticed.

Love felt like a currency
I never had enough of,
A language I could hear
but couldn't speak.

I kept trying to hand you
versions of myself
wrapped in gold silence,
hoping one of them
might finally
be enough.

And still,
some echoes follow me—
not as weight,
but residue—
the way air changes
in a place
you learned to hold your breath.

Fragile

I thought growing older
meant growing larger—
like the world would finally
make space
for the sound of me.

But instead,
I've become paper
in a city of stone.

Thin,
foldable,
always one gust away
from being scattered.

Everyone else
seems carved—
confident in the angles
they take up.
Unmoving.
Unbothered.

And I,
I drift.
I shrink myself in rooms
where certainty speaks too loud.
I second-guess my shadow.
I nod
when I mean
"no".

My spine bends
not from age
but from the weight
of never feeling
enough.

I used to believe,
I'd rise into myself—
that becoming
was something loud,
something visible.

But most days,
I just try to stand
without apology,

even if no one sees.

And sometimes,
that small defiance
is its own kind
of becoming.

Senior Year

I feel like a book
with the pages out of order—
the story moves,
but nothing lands
where it should.

My body is a hallway
I walk through quietly,
careful not to touch the walls,
not to wake whatever lives
behind them.

People talk to me
like I'm already here,
but I feel half-formed
like clay that never made it
to the kiln.
I'm soft in places
that should feel solid.
Missing in ways
no one else seems to notice.

I wear clothes
like disguises,
layer after layer
to cover a shape
that doesn't speak
the language of me.

Every mirror is a window
into someone else's life
I look in,
but don't recognize the scenes.
I wave,
no one waves back.

It's not pain,
not exactly—
just a constant itching
under the skin.
A knowing
with nowhere to go.

If someone asked what I'm
running from,
I wouldn't have an answer.
I just know

I'm always tired
and I'm never home.

And there's a name
for what this is—
I can feel it hovering
just beyond my breath.
But I can't reach it,
can't speak it,
so I carry it
like a secret
even I haven't been told.

Overcoming

I am not who I was
in the moments that broke me.
But I am also not
what those moments tried to make of me.

For a long time,
I mistook survival for numbness—
thought healing meant
not feeling anything at all.

But I was wrong.
Healing is messy.
It stings.
It wakes you up
when you just want to rest.

Some days, I move forward
without grace.
Some days, I am all hesitation,
all breath held too long.
But still,
I move.

There is strength—
In soft steps,
In showing up
even when your hands are shaking.

I'm not looking to become someone new.
But remembering
the parts of me
I had to set down
to survive.

Silly Me

You really thought
it meant something, didn't you?
The way time softened
just enough to let you breathe.
The way your chest felt
lighter, from being seen
without having to explain,
anything at all.

You held that moment
like it was rare—
like it had weight.
Laughter spilling out of you
so freely, you forgot
how often you keep yourself quiet.

You noticed the way their eyes lingered,
the warmth in their voice,
how their words curved
like they were shaping a space
for you to belong in.

It felt safe.
Effortless.
Like for once,
you didn't have to shrink
to fit.

And now here you are,
replaying it again
and again,
trying to figure out
how something that felt
so whole to you
left nothing in their hands.

You keep wondering
if they think of it at all.
If they ever sit in silence
and feel the whispers
you still carry.

But deep down—
you already know.
It was just you.
You were the only one

who stayed in that moment
long after it ended.

Strength

You've been through more
than most people could hold
without breaking—
but you didn't break.
You bent.
You were bruised.
You vanished for a while.
But you didn't disappear.

There are stories
carved in your silence
that no one will ever fully know.
And still,
you wake up
and try again.

That's strength.

You've walked through fire
disguised as friendship,
as love,

as safety,
and you made it out
even when the exit
was hard to find.

You've learned how to be
your own shelter.
How to sit with pain
without letting it
redefine you.

So if today
you feel small,
or tired,
or invisible,
let me remind you—

Surviving what you did
is its own kind of brilliance.

You are not behind.
You are not too much.
You are not lost.

You are a quiet force—

still unfolding,
and that alone
is enough
to be proud of.

I Carry You

I wasn't there
for the ordinary days
which led to the last.
Wasn't in the kitchen,
or the yard,
or the quiet moments
when presence
might have mattered more
than anything said.

I stayed away—
not out of apathy,
but something harder
to explain.
The kind of distance
you don't always choose,
but end up living in
until it's too late
to cross it.

You left,
before I could return.

Before I could sit beside you
without the weight of time
pressing so hard against my chest.

I keep thinking—
I should've come sooner.
I should've asked more questions.
Watched you from close.
Laughed longer.
Held you tighter.

Now, I carry you
like a photograph
tucked into a book
I never finished reading.
And I wonder
what you'd see
if you looked at me now.

Would you be proud
of the way I've grown?
Would you recognize the
quiet strength,
which took me years to build?
Would you know

I carry you
in all the ways
I try to show up better
than I did before?

Underneath

For a long time,
I thought it was anger—
sharp, fast,
always ready.

I carried it like a match
struck too easily,
burning before I could name
what I really felt.

But when I finally
sat still long enough
to stop sparking,
to stop defending,
I saw it—
the softer thing
beneath the flame.

It wasn't rage.
It was hurt
with no place to land.
It was fear,

wearing a louder coat.
It was grief,
disguised
as something easier to carry.

Anger was just
the only emotion
that didn't make me feel
exposed.
The only one
that made me feel
strong
when everything else
made me cave in.

But I'm learning
how to listen
to what comes before the fire—
the ache,
the ache,
the ache.

And now,
when I feel the heat rise,
I try to ask

what's underneath it.
What needs to be held
instead of silenced.
What needs to be heard
before it turns to flame.

The fire was never the threat—
just the signal.
A flare from the parts of me
still waiting
to be tended
instead of tamed.

Because maybe
I was never angry.
Maybe,
I was just
unseen.

Where It Lived

Grief doesn't arrive
out of empty air—
it grows
where something once rooted.

It's the overgrown garden
you keep forgetting to water,
but can't bear
to tear out.

The chair still pulled out
like someone's coming back.
The window left cracked
because they once liked the breeze.

It is the echo
of a name
you no longer say out loud,
but still hear
in the corners of quiet rooms.

Grief isn't absence.

It's evidence.
It is the dust
left behind
after light moves through a space.
The shape of something sacred
that once lived there,
still hovering
in the air it changed.

It only stays
because it once belonged.
Not as a wound,
but as a reminder—
that something lived here
and dared
to be felt
all the way through.

The Space You Left

The house changed
when you weren't in it anymore.

I noticed the way the fridge
sounded louder at night.
The way the couch kept its shape.
How your side of the closet
held only air.

I tried rearranging furniture
like that could shift something
inside of me.
But no matter where I moved
the damn lamp,
the floor still felt uneven.

I left your mug on
the counter for weeks
because putting it away
felt like admitting something
I still wasn't ready to say out loud.

And the worst part
wasn't the absence.
It was how the ordinary
kept going.
How the mail still came.
How the blinds still opened
like nothing had changed.

But everything had.
Yet I was the only one
left
to feel it.

Uneven Ground

Lately, life feels like a sidewalk
poured just slightly off balance—
enough to keep walking,
but never without noticing
the tilt.

The days stack up
like dishes in the sink—
evidence that I'm here,
that I'm trying,
even when it doesn't look like much.

Sometimes I laugh
and it feels honest.
Sometimes I laugh
and it feels like maintenance.

I scroll past people building lives
like skyscrapers
while mine still feels
like scaffolding—
bare bones and hope.

I've stopped chasing the finish line.
Now I just want to know
how to feel at home
in the middle of things.

In the unanswered messages,
in the quiet victories
no one claps for.

And maybe this is what becoming is—
not fire, not flight,
but learning to sit
in an unfinished room
and call it mine.

The Shape Of Your Soul

Are you kind to the waiter
when your food comes late?
Do you say "thank you"
like you mean it?
Do you hold the door
for strangers who won't notice?

I don't care about your angles.
I want to know the shape
of your thoughts
at 2 a.m.
when the world is quiet
and no one's watching.

Where's your favorite spot
to watch the sunset?
Do you wait for it
like a ritual,
or does it catch you off guard
every single time?

Do you have a love story

with the moon?
Do you look up
when life feels small
just to remember
how big it all actually is?

I want to know
what wrecked you
and what made you softer.

What songs you keep
for rainy drives.
What memory you carry
like a prayer.

Pretty fades.
But presence stays.
And I'm not asking
if you're flawless—
I'm asking
if you feel.
If you listen.
If you care.

Because the most beautiful

people I know don't need
the room to look at them—
they just make it feel
like home.

The Quiet I Had To Find

There were days
the world felt like too much air
and not enough breath.
Like I was walking through myself
but never arriving anywhere.

I wore my smile
like a borrowed jacket—
something to keep me warm
just long enough
to not be questioned.

Inside,
there were places
I wouldn't even visit alone.
Rooms with no windows,
just echoes
and too many locks.

Some nights,
it took everything

just to stay.
But I stayed.

Even when my hands shook
from holding on.
Even when I didn't believe
there was something better
on the other side of the silence.

I learned to listen
to what I used to outrun.
To sit with the ache
instead of hiding it
in the shadows.

Unraveling wasn't easy.
It never is, right?
But piece by piece,
I softened.
I named things I once feared
would swallow me whole.

And somewhere in that mess,
I found a voice
that didn't tremble.

A stillness
that wasn't absence,
but peace
I had earned
inch by inch.

Now,
when the dark comes,
I don't run—
I rest.
Because I am no longer
a war zone.

I am the quiet
I had to fight for.
And I am still here
to feel it.

If You Let Me

I'd lay the world at your feet
in pieces
I've collected quietly:
the softest sunrise I ever saw,
a street light flickering in the rain,
the sound a book makes
when it closes after healing you.

I want to know
how you take your coffee
and how you carry your sorrow.
Which days you need space
and which days you just need
someone to stay.

I don't want just your smile.
I want the story behind it.
The chapter you almost skipped.
The sentence that saved you.

I want to love you
like a lighthouse loves the lost

without asking
why they drifted in the first place.

Let me be the warmth
on your worst day.
The hand you don't have to reach for,
because it's already there.
Let me be the quiet
you come home to
when the world forgets how to listen.

Some people fall in love
like they're holding their breath.
I fall
like it's the only way
to come alive.

If you let me,
I'll love you
in every language
the sky has ever spoken.

And if I'm honest,
I want the kind of forever
where your hand finds mine

without thinking.
Where we grow into the quiet
without growing apart.
Where staying
isn't a promise—
it's just what we do.

Rising From the Ashes

I wasn't supposed
to survive this.
Not the weight,
not the silence,
not the way everything I loved
was taught to leave.

But I did.

Not gracefully,
not all at once,
but in pieces.
In mornings
I didn't believe I deserved.
In nights
I held myself together
because no one else knew how.

They don't tell you
that rising feels like breaking
again and again
until a shape that

finally fits your name.

There were versions of me
that burned
so another could breathe.
There were years
I mistook pain for identity
and stayed in rooms
that swallowed me whole.

But I kept going.
Not because I had the strength—
but because something inside me
refused to forget
what light felt like.

I rose
through ash,
through pain,
through the softest parts of me
that never stopped believing
I could begin again.

This isn't victory.
It's becoming.

It’s what happens
when a soul chooses
not to disappear.

Respectfully

I wasn't built
to make you comfortable.
Not anymore.

There were years I bit my tongue
until it bled
just to keep the peace.
Years I shaped myself
to fit inside rooms
that never made room for me.

But I burned that version.
The one who smiled through erasure,
who made themselves small
just to be allowed to stay.

Now I speak softer—
not because I'm unsure,
but because I no longer
need to shout
to know I exist.

I move through the world
without explanation.
Without apology.

If you don't understand me,
that's okay.
I didn't come here
to be explained.
I came here
to live.

Becoming Whole

I used to think healing
would feel like light—
like waking up clean,
untouched,
new.

But healing feels more like
remembering.
Like gathering pieces
you once called broken,
and realizing
they were always parts of the shape.

It's slow.
It's uneven.
It's learning to sit beside
the past
without letting it speak for you.

It's laughing
without flinching.
Crying

without shame.
Telling the truth
without needing it
to be palatable.

Becoming whole
doesn't mean going
back to who I was
before the break.
It meant learning to love
who I became
because of it.

I am not untouched.
But I am intact.
Not perfect,
but present.

And for the first time—
I don't need to be
anything else.

Thank You

I don't say it enough—
thank you
to the version of me
who stayed
when leaving felt easier.

The one who sat
in the wreckage
and dared to sort through it,
who reached for light
before knowing
if it would reach back.

Thank you
for walking into the fires
of your own becoming,
for asking the hard questions,
for learning how to breathe
without apology.

Because of you,
my days are quieter now—

not empty,
just gentle.
I wake up
and the weight isn't gone,
but it no longer
owns me.

There's color in the smallest things.
Warm tea,
sunlight on the floor,
a laugh I didn't expect.
And I know how to hold them now.
How to let joy stay.

I look in the mirror
and I recognize myself.
Not perfectly.
But truthfully.
And that's more than enough.

So here's to you—
the past me,
the hurting me,
the hopeful me.

You made this life possible.
And I won't waste
a single breath
of what you fought for.

Blank Pages

It used to come like weather-
a sonnet slipped beneath the door
before I even reached.

Now,
the sky inside me
is dry.
Cloudless.
Still.

I sit at the edge
of the same blank page
as if it might remember
how to speak
before I do.

Once,
my thoughts came dressed in rhythm-
syllables lining up
like constellations.
Now I reach for stars
but barely grasp the air.

The pen feels heavier now-
when there's nothing
to give it.
Like dragging a net
through water that refuses
to hold any shape.

There's a silence now
that isn't peace.
It's the kind that settles
in rooms you used to love.

I am waiting for the flicker,
for the heat inside my ribs,
the small voice that once
tapped so gently.

Somewhere,
beneath the silence,
beneath the dust
gathered on my imagination,
I believe the fire
is just sleeping.

So, I stay close,
listening for
the crackle.

She Knows

The Moon does not speak,
but she listens–
like an old friend
on the other end
of an unspoken prayer.

She wears silver
like sorrow
wears memory,
graceful and glowing
in the echo of every goodbye.

Each night,
she peels back
the sky and
steps barefoot
across the stars,
leaving soft footprints
in the dark that
we try to navigate.

We look up,

searching for answers
in her pale hush.
Though she never replies,
we still somehow understand.

She has seen
lovers break
and worlds begin,
Wars rage
and lullabies hum.

Still, she rises.
Still, she reflects what
little light she can gather,
and offers it gently
to those in need.

A quiet guardian
for the sleepless,
the dreamers,
and the ones
still learning
how to glow
in the absence
of the sun.

Leaving

I packed my life
into boxes that didn't
close properly,
dragged memories behind me
like loose threads,
and pointed myself
toward a new horizon
I couldn't see clearly.

There's no handbook
for leaving everything
you've known when you're
no longer twenty,
but not yet old enough
to wear your scars like wisdom.

I'm somewhere between
the reckless hunger
of beginnings and the steady
ache of knowing better—
Too seasoned to start
over clean.

Too restless to stay still.

The road didn't feel like
freedom at first—
It felt like grief.
Like letting go of ghosts
I thought I might need
again someday.

But somewhere between
state lines, I realized—
I wasn't chasing a new life.
I was unearthing the one
that was buried under
all the lives I lived
for everyone else.

It's strange,
carving out a new home
in your thirties,
strange how the silence
feels louder when you're
supposed to know
yourself by now.

But maybe this is the real knowing—
Standing in the middle of nowhere,
half-built, half-broken,
hands opens, saying,
This is still for me.

And If I am a map,
then every wrong turn,
every small heartbreak,
every burning bridge—
They brought me here.
Not late.
Not lost.
Just finally arriving.

Belonging

There's a loneliness
they don't tell you about–
the kind that follows you
even when you're the one
choosing to leave.

It lives in the first nights,
when the city outside
hums in a language
you haven't yet learned.
When you move through
your own space like
a guest.

Starting over isn't a clean break–
It's a slow, invisible tear.
A shedding you can't rush
without losing pieces you
may still need.

Fitting in feels like
folding myself into

new shapes,
practicing until it
doesn't feel like
pretending.
Some days,
I miss the version of me
who didn't know how
heavy freedom could be.

I'm learning that belonging
is not a place.
It's the slow stitching
of small moments
into the fabric of
a life you claim
even when no one's
watching.

A Strange Kind of Gravity

There's a darkness
I don't always talk about—
the kind that doesn't howl
or scream,
but sits quietly
at the base of my ribs,
shaping the way
I move through the world.

My mind doesn't walk
the way others do.
It drags,
it claws,
it spins in quiet storms
most people can't hear.

I feel things
too deeply,
so they tell me—
like it's an apology
I should make

for every room
I couldn't float through
lightly enough.

Joy and sorrow
aren't opposites here.
They blur together,
wearing each other's clothes.
Even laughter sometimes
feels like an ache
dressed in bright colors.

This depth
isn't a choice—
it's a strange kind of gravity,
pulling everything inside me
toward the center
until it's too heavy to carry,
but too much a part of me
to set down.

There are days
when the light feels
like something sharp,
not something warm.

Days where even
tenderness stings.

And still,
I wake.
I breathe.
I carry it.
All of it.
Because somehow,
even the weight
has taught me
ways to stay.

The Way We Tell It.

Poetry softens the sharp edges,
paints the grief gold,
puts the heaviest ache
into a smaller, more beautiful cage.

I say "the night cracked open"
instead of admitting
I couldn't sleep
because I was afraid
of my own mind.
I say "the stars wept"
instead of telling you
it was me,
folded in half
on the bathroom floor.

In poetry,
loneliness becomes a room
I choose to walk into.
In poetry,
loss has a softer name.

It isn’t dishonesty.
It’s survival.
It's how we make sense
of being ripped open
in places no one can see.

Poetry isn’t always
the way it happened.
But it’s always
the way it felt.
And sometimes,
that’s the only truth
that matters.

Atmosphere

Don't ask me what I am—
I've shed too many skins to keep score.
Today I am mist at the throat of a mountain,
tomorrow I'll be a storm
with no memory of calm.

I've lived as wind
threading through keyholes,
as thunder breaking
in the bones of the bold.
Once, I was a mirage
and watched them drink
from the thirst I left behind.

I arrive without a pattern,
a flicker between forms.
They try to forecast me
in skies I outgrow—
every label crumbles
under the weight of my maybe.

I am not just becoming.

I am undoing.
A slow unspooling
of every shape I was told to keep.
To meet me
is to feel the air change.
And even then,
you'll only know the weather,
never the atmosphere it came from.

The Way the Night Spoke

Last night,
the sky leaned low enough
I thought I could climb it,
step into its hollow throat,
and walk toward something
I've been chasing without knowing.

The streets were emptied of names,
only the whisper of distant windows—
lives stacked like forgotten books.
I carried my wanting carefully,
like a match in the wind.

Somewhere beyond these miles,
someone was turning off their lamp,
dragging a blanket over tired legs,
not knowing they were the gravity
I had been circling all along.

I passed a garden
where the flowers slept open-mouthed,

a stray cat curling into the shape
of something forgiven,
and for a moment,
the whole night
felt full of messages
I wasn't brave enough to read.

I have no GPS for this.
Only a pulse that quickens
at the thought of meeting someone
who might already be dreaming of me—
softly,
without meaning to,
without knowing yet
where to find my voice.

As the Forest Does

I am learning to change
as the forest does—
not in haste,
but in increments too soft to measure.

Once, I believed evolution was eruption,
a shedding of skin ablaze.
But now I see
how even trees grow
by fractions,
how moss does not ask
permission to bloom.

There are days I feel barren,
stripped by unseen seasons—
but even that is nature,
the bark breaks
so that light can enter.

Growth is not always graceful.
It is root-deep,
a reaching through dark soil

toward something
you don't yet believe in.
The earth turns,
the sap rises,
and I too,
begin again—
quietly becoming
what I could not even name before.

The Museum of Molting Things

They told me to evolve,
so I went underground.

Not a metaphor—
I mean I crawled into the hollows
where truth drips from the ceiling
and time gathers like condensation
on the backs of forgotten teeth.

There were others here—
not people,
but, not creatures exactly,
something between shedding and arrival.
Their eyes were closed,
but their dreams moved the walls.

I found a sign that read:
"Exhibit Closed for Reformation."
Still, the walls pulsed with a heartbeat
that sounded so familiar.
I peeled off my expectations

like wet fabric.
Hung my name beside the others.
Let my spine coil
into the shape of a question
I wouldn't dare ask aloud.

Every seven days,
my shadow splits from me
and walks in circles,
whispering updates
from the life I abandoned above.

Sometimes I could smell rain
through the floor.
Other times,
I swore I saw a version of myself
with wings
trapped inside the amber
of a thought I never had.

Eventually,
my bones softened.
My shape forgot its purpose.
I became an echo
that hadn't happened yet.

And when I surfaced,
the sky didn't recognize me—
but the birds did.
They called me something
I couldn't translate.
But it felt right.
Like a name meant to be worn
inside the skin.

Tear It Down To Be Free

I was born in a house with no door.
No windows,
only walls that cringed
when I got too close to the truth.

They said it was mine.
That I'd always lived there.
But the ceiling changed colors
when I asked for my name,
and the floors pulsed
like somthing trying to remember
being alive.

At night, paintings appeared—
portraits of people
with my eyes
and no mouths.
I stared until they wept.
They wept until I understood
the cost of silence.

Sometimes I'd find glass

under my tongue,
or salt in my pockets
with no ocean to explain it.

There was a mirror,
but it only showed the version of me
that never made the safe choice.

I envied him.

He had scars I couldn't trace,
and a softness I didn't deserve.

The walls grew tighter each year.
Eventually, I began to shrink
to fit their idea of me.
My voice grew roots
and sank beneath the floorboards.
My shadow forgot how to follow.

One morning,
the house opened its chest
and said:
"If you want to leave,
you must unbuild me."

So, I began.

Ripping wallpaper woven of memories.
Breaking beams carved from belief.
Peeling paint made of promises
I never meant to keep.

Beneath it all—
a field
Untouched.

And in the center,
a child
carving a door into the air.
He turned and stretched
his hand out to me,
like he had been waiting
his whole life,
for me to set him free.

The Lines That Hold Me Together

Once,
I shattered so quietly
the world didn't notice.

The breaking was not a scream—
it was a hush,
a slipping between layers,
a crumbling that started in the softest
marrow.

I gathered myself in handfuls—
splinters of bone,
ribbons of breath,
small chambers of once-bright things.

There was no healer,
no ceremony.
Only these hands,
clumsy with grief,
learning how to lace gold
through the ruins without asking

if they deserved to shine.

I stitched myself
with molten hope,
threaded seams so bright
the night leaned closer
just to see them.

Now, when you touch me,
you won't find smoothness.
You will find rivers,
trembling veins of what refused to die,
running between the wreckage.
I am not new.
I am not whole in the way you think.
But every crack sings louder
than the stone ever could.

Slow & Steady

It won't be a grand arrival.
No thunderclap.
No sweeping declarations
in crowded rooms.

It'll happen the way fog
finds a shoreline—
so slowly
you don't notice at first
how everything
feels softer
because of it.

One evening,
your voice will fill a silence
I didn't realize
I had been afraid of.
Not by rushing in—
but by sitting there,
patiently,
unmovingl,
until even the quiet

felt different.

I won't know the moment
your laugh
became the thing
I look for in a room.
Or the day
I stopped wondering
how far you'd stay.

There won't be sparks,
not the kind that dazzle and die.
There will be something steadier—
a light you can read by,
a hand you recognize in the dark
because it's always been there,
even before you knew
to reach for it.

And one morning,
without meaning to,
I'll make coffee for two
before I remember
it was never a promise—
only a hope

you kept choosing
slowly,
quietly,
and all the same,
still.

Everyone Looks Beautiful in the Dark

There's glitter ground into the carpet,
half a pizza sliding off the counter,
someone swaying with their eyes closed
like the music might hold them up.

I sit on the edge of the couch,
a plastic cup sweating in my hands,
pretending to text,
pretending there's someone on the other end.
Someone bumps into me—
too much perfume,
a mouth full of apologies,
then they're gone,
folded back into the pulse of bodies
spilling from room to room.

I tell myself I'm just tired.
That maybe the night
got too loud too fast.
That maybe if I stay
just a little longer,

the feeling will catch up.

Out back,
a group huddles around a lighter,
faces lit up
like paper lanterns
about to tear.

Inside,
someone's laughing so hard they're choking.
Someone's spilling beer on the carpet.
Someone's kissing someone else's ex.
Everyone looks beautiful in the dark.
Everyone seems to know
exactly who they are,
exactly where to put their hands.

I find the bathroom,
lock the door,
sit on the edge of the tub
just to hear myself breathe.
The music leaks through the walls,
low and distant,
like a memory
I was never part of.

I stay there
until the silence feels heavier
than the noise.

Then I wash my face,
wipe my hands on my jeans,
and go back out.
No one notices.
That's the best part.
No one notices at all.

5:45PM

Some nights,
I trace the places you aren't.
Press my palm up to the
doorframe you once
leaned against—
Half-asleep, half-smiling,
waiting for my warm embrace.

The sky fades too fast these days.
The light just doesn't linger
the way it used to.
It stretches thin,
then just vanishes.
Poof.
No apology.
No sound.

I sit out on the porch anyway,
letting the night settle
against my skin.
Waiting for a sound that
just isn't going to come.

No shutting car door.
No footsteps.
No laughter.
Just the soft breathing
of a world
I still have to face.

The Way the Light Moves

There's a stretch of road
where the trees lean in just enough
to make you feel held.
Where the sky breaks open
into small, patient pieces
and you forget you're in a rush.

I drove it yesterday,
windows down,
hands trailing out like I could catch
something invisible but certain.
The fields hummed low and steady,
crickets stitching the edges of the air,
the sun slipping itself gently
onto every surface it could find.

No one tells you how rare it is—
to feel full without wanting more,
to look out at a place
and know it owes you nothing,
yet still gives you everything.

I wanted to bottle it—
the sway of tall grass,
the soft crack of gravel under tires,
the way my chest felt
both wide open
and steady for once.

There was no soundtrack,
no camera flash.
Just a breeze threading
through the seams
of a tired sweatshirt,
and the quiet certainty
that for a moment,
the world had nothing to take
and everything to offer.

What's Safer?

There's a page torn from a notebook
buried somewhere in my glove box.
It's nothing—
just your name,
drawn a few times,
once with a heart over the i
before I realized what I was doing.

I didn't crumple it.
Didn't throw it out.
I just closed the glove box like closing a thought.
Like sliding a feeling down into
something quieter than it wanted to be.

You were a Tuesday.
A joke told too late at night.
A hand brushing mine
on accident,
or maybe not.

The kind of closeness

you can't explain to anyone else
because it sounds like nothing
unless you were there.

And you were there.

I keep thinking
there's a version of this
where I say too much,
where it spills out in the wrong place,
where it scares you away.

So I don't say anything.
I leave it in the glove box.
I leave it between breaths.
I leave it where things stay small
because small
feels safer
than broken.

The World Is Art

I used to think that art
lived in sketchbooks
and concert halls.
In hands that knew
how to hold instruments
or pencils.
I thought it had edges,
Rules,
A frame.

But I've seen the sky
blush at 6:14am,
and I know better now.

Art is the way sun
spills through the blinds
onto someone's shoulder
when they're still half asleep.
It's the bruise-colored sky
before the storm.
It's poetry written in silence,
Without rhyme,

without reason,
Just truth.

Art is making dinner for one
and lighting a candle anyway.
It's letting someone in when
you don't know how to
explain the mess.
It's laughter breaking
in the middle of grief.
It's choosing softness.

Art is a night in.
It's staying when fear
is telling you to run.
It's the questions we keep
asking ourselves without
seeking any answers.

I used to think art
had to be made.
Now I know—
Sometimes,
it only needs
to be noticed.

The Biggest Part of Me, My Best Friend

We didn't have places
so much as excuses.
You'd text me the name of a store—
somewhere safe to say you were—
and I'd pull into the lot,
windows down,
engine humming low like a secret.

You'd slip into the passenger seat,
no groceries, no questions,
just that quick look we always shared—
the one that said I get it
without needing to explain a thing.

Sometimes we rode bikes
until the tires went soft with heat,
until our shadows stretched too thin across
the asphalt.
We'd leave them in weeds by the train tracks,
walking side by side
like the whole world could balance itself

on two worn–out sneakers.

We talked about nothing
and everything.
About the houses we couldn't breathe in,
about futures we couldn't yet name.
Our voices were just small enough
to slip under the noise of passing cars,
just loud enough
to promise we were still here.

You never had to say you needed out—
your headlights in the lot told me.
My open door told you.

We made a map out of nowhere.
Out of gravel and headlights and summer
heat.
Out of songs half–sung and
soda bottles left under car seats.

It was never about the tracks,
the cover stories,
the blistering winter cold...
It was about finding someone

who didn't need you to explain
why you showed up late,
why your voice cracked,
why you stayed longer than
you said you would.

You are the only place
I have ever arrived at
without getting lost first.

Do You Ever Wonder?

Do you ever wonder
what happens when our light burns out?
When the weight of breath leaves us,
and we are nothing but energy
unspooling into something vaster
than we can name?

Do we drift,
untethered,
into the cold eternal dark,
our shapes folding into the void
like smoke lost in an endless sky?

Or are we met—
arms open,
familiar faces gathering like stars,
pulling us into a warmth
we once forgot
but somehow always knew?

Is the pain washed away?
The old aches and heavy shadows

peeled off of us
like worn skin,
left behind the door
of some gentler place?

Or do we begin again,
without memory,
without mourning,
stepping onto another stage,
into another name,
wearing new hands,
new hearts,
playing roles we do not recognize
but feel, somehow, as ours?

I wonder if the soul remembers
what the mind is made to forget.
If some part of us lingers—
a thread of knowing stitched deep.

It's Probably Nothing

Sometimes,
I catch someone's eyes
and can't tell if it's desire
or dissection.

A glance held a second too long—
not enough to call it anything,
but just enough
to make my skin breed
the question:
what do they see?

Do they notice
the slope of my jaw
before I do?
Do they trace the old blueprint
beneath my clothes,
the one I try not to feel
when mirrors forget to be kind?

I shift my shoulders,
deepen my voice without meaning to.
There's a reflex

to pass,
to disappear,
to appear
just right.

Even on the good days,
the ones where I feel solid,
where my name sits comfortably
in someone's mouth—
there's still that flicker,
that flash of wondering
if I'm being read
or revealed.

It's like walking through a world
that keeps holding up x-rays
when all I wanted
was to be seen in color.

And maybe they're just looking.
Maybe it's nothing.
But when your body's been
a battleground,
you learn to read stares
like survival manuals.

Still,
I hold my head up.
I let them look.
I remind myself—
whatever they see
can't touch what I've
built underneath.

Illness

You are the kind of person
who speaks softly to everyone,
waves at dogs,
says "thank you" like it's sacred.

You've built your whole life
out of quiet goodness—
never asking for credit,
never needing to be right,
just steady,
and kind,
and present.

So, when they said
you were the one who
might not be okay—
my stomach dropped
like it had no floor to land on.

It didn't make sense.
It still doesn't.

Out of everyone,
you?

You who held the world gently,
even when it didn't return the favor.
You, who made mistakes feel like lessons,
who taught me what grace looks like
without ever needing the word.

I didn't know what to do with it.
How to carry a fear
that big and that silent.
How to hold space for someone
who always made space for me.

I wanted to scream
at whatever force decided
that someone like you
should have to fight
just to keep being here.

But I didn't scream.
I stayed still,
out of reverence,
out of shock,

out of not knowing
what to do with the kind of fear
that feels too fragile to say out loud.

All Good

It's fine.
Really.
No hard feelings when the
hope is this small,
easy to hide
in the pocket of a jacket
I never take off anyway.

You don't owe me a thing.
Not your time,
not your noticing.
I knew better.
But still—
hope has a way of slipping in
through the smallest cracks,
like light under a locked door
you can only dream of what's behind.

Still, it's funny—
how someone can become part of
your thinking without even trying.
How you start fixing your hair

for a conversation that never happens,
checking your reflection
in windows you were supposed to walk past.

There's a kind of harmlessness to it.
A little sting,
like biting your lip on accident—
You taste the blood,
you move on.
You don't cry over it.
You just press your tongue against it once,
and keep talking like it didn't happen.

Tomorrow,
I'll forget how carefully I
rehearsed things
you were never meant to hear.
I'll shake my head,
laugh under my breath,
the way you do when you trip
over nothing
and hope no one notices.

It's fine.
Really.

Some things are meant to stay soft—
a reminder that I can still feel,
that my heart is finally
opening up again,
after years of being hardened.

Even Shadows Need a Place to Rest

Even shadows
need a place to rest—
a soft stretch of wall,
a patch of ground
where they're not asked
to follow or flee.

They tire, too,
those silent echoes—
always trailing,
never leading,
never seen
until the light demands it.
I think of mine
sometimes—
how it clings to my heels,
how it carries
the weight of things
I pretend I've let go of.

And maybe

it wants to disappear
into the folds of dusk,
curl beneath the bones of a dying star,
float faceless
through the corridors of sleep
where no one asks it to be light.

Not all things ask for mending.
Some simply want
to drip like candle wax into the dark,
to be named only by the wind,
to belong to nothing—
and still be whole
in the absence of repair.

Even the quietest parts of us
deserve a home.
Even the dark
needs a little peace.

The Ghosts Don't Haunt Me, They Stay for Tea

They stopped slamming doors
a long time ago.
Stopped rattling windows,
whispering names
in the back of my mind.

Now they arrive
like old friends—
no knocking,
just the sound of settling
in the hollow parts of the room.

They sit in the chair
I always leave empty.
Sip from cups
I don't remember pouring.

We don't speak much anymore.
But sometimes
they hum songs I've forgotten,
or brush past me

just enough
to remind me they were real.

They don't scare me.
Not like before.
Not like when memory
felt like fire
and I kept reaching for it anyway.

Now,
they stay for tea.
They watch me write.
They nod when I pause.
And leave
just before the water goes cold.

Letter I Never Sent

I don't know why I'm writing this—
maybe to hold the weight of you
in something safer.

Sometimes I wonder
if we overthink it all
at the same time.
If, in the middle of chopping onions
or changing the sheets,
you stop—
not because of what you're doing,
but because the air
feels heavier all of a sudden,
a thought sat down beside you
without asking.

I think about you
in strange places.
In the way the wind
pushes against closed doors,
in the sudden silence
between two sentences

that never quite connect.

I don't reach out.
Neither do you.
But I wonder if we drift
along the same shoreline—
your feet in one tidepool,
mine in another,
still pulled
by the same moon.

You live in the pauses.
In the part of the song
where the instruments drop
and you wait for the words to return.

I keep wondering
if you ever half-type something,
then erase it.
If you hear your name
in someone else's voice
and it makes your stomach shift.
If you think about
what we could've been
in the soft light

before sleep dulls the wanting.

I don't need an answer.
I just needed to say—
some part of me
moves toward you
in ways I don't speak out loud.
You probably already know that.
Maybe you feel it
in the quiet
and just don't call it by name.

—me

Where the Pages Let Me Stay

I didn't know where to go
with the noise in my head,
the storm of almosts
and unfinished aches
spilling into every quiet moment.

So, I opened a notebook
and let it hold me.
No explanations.
No edits.
Just ink,
and space,
and the safety of not being watched.

I wrote my way
through rooms I never wanted to enter,
and out of corners
I didn't know I was hiding in.

Some days,
the words came slow—

like coaxing light through fog.
Other days,
they ran ahead of me,
laughing,
leaping onto the page
before I could catch up.

Each sentence
a small unpacking.
Each page
a door I didn't know I needed to open.
And somewhere between
the crossings-out and the margins,
I found a kind of peace
I hadn't felt in years.
A place that didn't ask me to be better,
just honest.

My notebooks became home—
not because they solved anything,
but because they let me stay
when I had nowhere else to put the weight.

An Absence With Teeth

It's not loneliness
like an empty chair
or silence after a goodbye.

It's more like
standing in a room
where the walls keeps shifting,
and none of the windows are real.

Like something is watching
from inside the mirror,
but refuses to speak.

I move through days
like smoke through keyholes—
barely touching anything,
but leaving a shape behind.

Even joy feels borrowed,
like someone else's coat
left on my shoulders
in the wrong season.

I want more—
but it's not hunger.
It's a thirst
with no mouth to drink from,
a compass spinning
in a world with no magnets.

At night,
my thoughts become birds
with no sky to climb—
just wings flapping
in the dark between stars
that won't give directions.

So I guess this is what it means
to live with a map
that keeps erasing itself
every time you think
you've found the path home.

Small Wish

I don't know what today looks like for you—
if the mirror was kind,
if the world let you exhale.
But I hope,
somewhere between your first sip
and the sound of morning settling in,
you felt beautiful.

Not for anyone else's eyes,
not because of a filter or a compliment—
but because something in you opened
just enough
to remember you are still evolving,
and still worthy
while doing it.

And I hope your coffee tastes great.
I hope it wraps around your hands
like a small promise—
a little warmth that belongs only to you.

Not everything needs to be profound.

Sometimes,
just feeling good for a moment
is a revolution.

Where Do We Belong?

Where the hell do hopeless romantics belong?
Do we sit in the ash
before anyone even lights the match?
Do we carry velvet hearts
in a world built for plastic ones—
fragile things
in hands that were never taught to hold
them?

Is our place at the diner booth at midnight,
food gone cold,
eyes fixed on the door
like we're waiting
for someone who only exists in poetry?

Do we stay up at 1am
talking to the ceiling,
yearning not for touch,
but for closeness that means something?
The kind that sees you
when you're not trying to be seen.
The kind that says,

"Stay",
without needing a reason.

We don’t want just anyone.
We want a soul
that rhymes with ours
in ways language can't explain.
Someone who listens
even when we speak in silence.

Sometimes it feels like
we’re relics from a different time—
tucked into this era by mistake,
trying to write sonnets
in a world that sends thumbs-up emojis
and calls it love.

So where do we belong?
Maybe nowhere.
Maybe everywhere.
Maybe we’re the ones
who keep love alive
by daring to believe
it still means something.